Safe as H

CHATTO
CounterBlasts

Margaret
DRABBLE

Safe as Houses

Chatto & Windus
LONDON

Published in 1990 by
Chatto & Windus Ltd
20 Vauxhall Bridge Road
London SW1V 2SA

A CIP catalogue record for this book
is available from the British Library

ISBN 0 7011 3553 0

Photoset in Linotron Ehrhardt by
Rowland Phototypesetting Ltd
Bury St Edmunds, Suffolk
Printed in Great Britain by
St Edmundsbury Press Ltd
Bury St Edmunds, Suffolk

THE IDEA FOR this CounterBlast dates back to 1988. A great deal has changed in the housing market since then.

Remember the summer of '88? House prices were soaring in a seemingly never-ending flight through the roof of possibility. Owners were secretly rubbing their hands with glee as their properties appreciated by the hour. Buyers were chasing round the country competing desperately for desirable or undesirable residences, many of them willing to pay well above the asking price. Estate agents were opening new branches in every high street in the land. Banks and building societies were vying with one another to offer tempting loans. 100 per cent mortgages were proliferating. Builders were building, developers were developing, speculators were speculating. Council tenants were buying their homes and lavishing love and care on new doors, porches, glazing and garden featues. There was a frenzy of activity that fed its own momentum. The turnover was tremendous, profits were spectacular. It was boom, boom, rush, rush, everywhere. Could this be quite what we wanted?

Not everyone was happy – first-time buyers on

small incomes saw even unconverted one-bedroom basement grottoes rise beyond their means, snapped up by those with more money to play with, those who could spend on damp courses and refurbishment, those who believed that any bit of dwelling space was an investment. Council tenants who could not afford to buy were not happy, as waiting lists lengthened and bed-and-breakfast hotels filled up. The roofless homeless, displaced or evicted from violent families, from childhood spent in care, from the emptying Victorian psychiatric hospitals and hostels and night shelters, were not happy. Local authorities, unable to meet their statutory obligations, unable to build, contemplated their diminishing housing stock with alarm. But by and large, back in 1988, most people were happy.

Most people still are happy, and let me make it clear at once that is not my purpose to argue against home ownership, or to try to suggest that more of the population is badly housed now than it was ten, twenty, or thirty years ago. Overall, housing conditions have improved, and expectations have risen accordingly. Most of those expectations are being fulfilled. We are happy in our homes, and most of us do not perceive that there is any kind of housing crisis. Housing is hardly on the political agenda, and there are no honours in it. Building Societies Association surveys indicate that there has been a steady increase in those expressing themselves 'very satisfied' with their housing (46 per cent in 1975, 52 per cent in 1986, 57 per cent in 1989). The total proportion of those 'dissatisfied' fell from 11 per cent to 4 per cent between 1975 and 1989. The 'quite satisfied', however, are decreasing – from 36 in 1986 to 33 in 1989. Some of the unhappier 3 per cent probably feature in the previous paragraph. (Mark Boléat, *Housing in Britain*, May 1989.)

But problems remain, apparently intransigent problems. The numbers of the homeless increase, there is a serious deficiency of cheap rented accommodation, either public or private, and building is at an all-time low. Although house prices have stuck, they have stuck at a level that makes it almost impossible for many first-time buyers to get their feet on the ladder. How is a young single woman, working in Greater London, in receipt of a wage of £9,5000, ever going to finance a one-bedroom flat or a so-called 'studio flat', even on a 100 per cent mortgage if she could get it on that income? (Prices start around £50,000: the average for a Greater London converted flat is £87,024, for a purpose-built £78,979: the figures for the Outer Metropolitan Area for the first quarter of 1990 are £66,063 and £64,389 respectively. Barry Bissett, Nationwide Anglia.) What are her options? To rent, to squat, to flat-share, to stay at home with Mum and Dad, to put her name on the council list?

What is a low-waged family in the south-east to do when a report commissioned by the House Builders Federation and the Association of District Councils concludes that 'the most characteristic product of the contemporary house building industry, a family house in south-east England, could not be afforded by 75 per cent of households living in that region' (February 1990)? And the prospect is, as we home owners are constantly reassured, that some time soon prices will begin to rise again, leaving these not particularly hard cases even further behind. No wonder people press for wage increases. And so the inflationary spiral continues . . .

There is something odd about a situation in which a government which believes in and promotes the idea of home ownership allows property prices to inflate beyond the means of many, and fails to take seriously the task of providing decent alternative accommodation. It is not only odd, it is illogical. Perhaps inflation in housing is thought to be different from inflation in the economy at large? Perhaps it is a Good Thing?

One of the glaring illogicalities of the present regime is its commitment to the vast concealed housing subsidy of mortgage interest tax relief, which now runs at some £6.75 billion a year. Of course, there are a lot of votes in this tax relief, and the more heavily-mortgaged home owners you have in the electorate, the more carefully you have to tread. The free market here might prove too expensive for any party. Nevertheless, some Tories, with admirable consistency, hanker after it – though not, it appears, Mrs Thatcher herself. Perhaps she prefers votes to consistency.

In the summer of 1988, an attempt was made to intervene against property inflation. On 1 August, multiple mortgage tax relief on a single property was abolished. Young couples fought their way past television cameras to building societies to place their deposits in the last half-hour of trading on 29 July. The date is burned into my building society passbook, for on this day I gave a young couple an emergency bridging loan to allow them to meet the deadline, and although it was instantly repaid I have been waiting nervously ever since to hear their reproaches for encouraging them to overstretch themselves. Luckily, with their combined income they can afford their dramatically increased mortgage payments. Well, they would be able to, wouldn't they? As it says in Matthew 25, 'Unto every one that hath shall be given' – or at least, to them it shall be at the last moment lent.

After this crucial date, the whole property market trembled and stuck. The third boom of the last two decades was over. Interest rates rose, month after

5

relentless month, ratcheting their way up by 3, by 4, by 5 per cent. The Gadarene rush to buy came to a sudden halt, and a lack of confidence spread through the market, infecting even those who had no interest in a double mortgage and who had no immediate intention of buying or selling. Maybe investing in property wasn't such a clever wheeze after all. Maybe one could come unstuck. Maybe one could get landed with a mortgage that would cost more than the value of one's home. Maybe one wouldn't be able to keep up payments. What if one suddenly had to move to a new job and had to sell at a loss? Maybe houses could actually, God forbid, *drop* in value. Maybe houses weren't as safe as houses. Maybe we should all just stay where we are.

Could *this* be quite what we wanted? Many thought not.

The media began to seize on hard-luck stories of council-house buyers furtively trying to resell to the council, of repossessions from over-extended first-time buyers who found themselves getting deeper and deeper into debt, on horror stories of councils having to buy back homes sold with serious structural defects. Mortgage defaulters were (and still are) news. Ruined estate agents made more jolly copy. Estate agents have always had a bad press and there was a malicious pleasure in accounts of closing branches and heavy losses. Serve them bloody right, was the general opinion. Builders and removal men, also badly hit, were treated with more sympathy. But by and large, the fall in house prices – or, more strictly, the arresting of the increase in the inflation of house prices – was perceived to be a Bad Thing, even by those who had recently been bewailing the fantastic profits and unreal prices of the year before. Words like 'slump' and 'crash' can never be intended as good news.

So what was it that we *did* want, then? Did we *want* prices to go on going up forever? *Could* they go on going up forever? Where did all that extra money *come from and go to?* Was it real? I found myself feeling a sneaking sympathy for Nigel Lawson. At least he'd had a go.

So, for the last two years, I've been keeping half an eye on the market, cutting out headlines from the property pages, and chatting to estate agents and housing departments of local authorities and housing trusts and charities for the homeless and quangos and council tenants and politicians. I started off with a fairly open mind and one or two hunches.

One hunch was that the level, or indeed the existence, of mortgage interest tax relief (currently set at £30,000, unchanged in the March 1990 budget despite lobbying for a higher ceiling) was inconsistent both with the government's own free-market policy and with my own sense of fair play.

I could understand (well, sort of) the reasoning that in 1965 exempted and continues to exempt first homes from Capital Gains Tax, but it seemed a nonsense that if I were rich enough to buy a second home, I could still keep tax relief on my so-called first home, and that I would indeed be advised to do so by my accountants. I could buy a subsidised motor car or a holiday in a health farm or a satellite dish with the relief. This was very nice, but was it what was intended? It is a fact that of the growing billions of hidden subsidy conceded annually by the Exchequer, the richest proportionately get the most. People like me didn't need a subsidy, we didn't need an encouragement to invest in property. We were home owners already. If we wanted to buy more, we could afford to do it unaided. Let help, in the government's own language, be targeted to those in need, not to the already affluent.

I suspected also that tax relief was in itself inflationary – and events following the summer of '88 proved me right. (I still don't understand why some property experts seem to think inflation in house prices is always such a Good Thing, and that it will make us all richer and richer forever. Am I being stupid?)

As I pursued this particular line of enquiry, I found I had some strange fellow travellers. The Duke of Edinburgh, Michael Meacher, Nigel Lawson, Shirley Williams, Michael Heseltine,

Paddy Ashdown, John Biffen, the Bow Group, the *New Statesman*, and rightwing sociologist Professor Peter Saunders had all for different and sometimes opposing reasons shared my doubts about the wisdom of mortgage interest tax relief, though some of them, under electoral pressure, had been forced hastily to abandon them. (Paddy Ashdown, the professor, and as far as I know the duke have all stuck to their guns. One doesn't have to ponder long to see why.) I began to think that perhaps NOBODY really thinks MITR is in the long run, for the nation as a whole, a Good Thing. Perhaps everybody agrees with the proposition that 'the incidence of help given by tax relief is grotesque in its excessive assistance to those least in need' (H. Aughton, *Housing Finance, A Basic Guide*, Shelter, 1981), or with the Bow Group, which argued, more obscurely, that MITR discouraged home ownership. Either way, nobody seems to know how to get rid of it.

(You *can* get rid of tax relief. Remember the days back in the forgotten sixties when you got tax relief on the interest of any sum borrowed for any purpose? Fur coats, motor cars, racehorses, bathroom extensions, the lot? This relief was abolished in 1969 by a Labour government, which made a deliberate decision to exempt mortgage interest payments. If there was an indignant outcry, we have forgotten it. Car sales slowed momentarily,

but one could hardly suggest they haven't recovered
– alas, as Jonathon Porrit might say.)

I also suspected that housing does not respond
like other commodities to the usual laws of supply
and demand. On closer examination, I think I am
right. I am no economist, but even I can tell that a
home is a different *kind* of commodity from a car
or a video machine or a saucepan or a hamburger
or a three-piece suite.

1. A home takes longer to make and occupies
more space than any other item of normal personal
expenditure, and thus has a different relationship
to time and space, to long-term finance and to
long-term planning. In the present state of building
technology, if we need new houses, we can't build
them overnight, and we can't import them. Space
is by its nature and by law limited and with green
thinking is becoming more, not less so.

2. A home costs more than any other item of
personal expenditure, unless you move up into the
executive jet, steam-yacht, diamond tiara, old-
master level.

3. Unlike other common consumer durables, a
house appreciates in value, sometimes as spectacularly as an old master. The vast majority of houses
sold are not new but second, third, or thirtieth
hand, and some of the oldest are some of the most
valuable. A house can be, in Fred Hirsch's term,

a positional good. It can also, more usually, be a safe-as-houses investment, far safer than stocks and shares.

These factors – and there are probably others – alter the nature of the home as commodity. A home is not an exchangeable, inevitably deteriorating, eventually replaceable possession, like an electric toaster or a helicopter. Nor is it an appreciating Impressionist painting. It is different in kind.

Buying a house is not a simple economic trans-action. It involves more of us, more of us as people, both as idiosyncratic individuals and as basic eco-nomic units, than any other purchase we are likely to make in a lifetime. It makes us behave worse than any other kind of transaction we are likely to make, perhaps because more depends on it. Where else would we lie and cheat and gazump and back out of contracts and bid up at auctions and waste the time and money of others as regularly, as selfishly, as guiltlessly, as we do over housing? It may be that we behave so badly because so much money is involved – for most of us, a lifetime's investment, a lifetime's savings. A mistake in a house purchase is serious and long lasting, and we should all welcome controls to compel estate agents and surveyors and prospective buyers and pur-chasers to behave responsibly and pay for their own negligence or deceit or hesitations.

But it may be that other factors also operate. Let us look at the new political mystique of home ownership, and see if it offers any clues either to the inconsistencies of our own attitudes or to what is now happening both to the housed and to the homeless. It may also throw light on the relationship between the two.

The British, as is well known, stand fairly high in the world stakes of home ownership – not as high as the Bangladeshis, but appreciably higher than, for example, the Germans, the Swiss, the French, the Swedes and the Dutch. This is not a new Thatcherite phenomenon. It is deep rooted. Home ownership in this country has been growing steadily, encouraged in various ways by successive governments, at the expense of the private rented sector, since the end of the First World War. By the end of 1988 we had reached a position where 65.4 per cent of homes were owner-occupied, and 81 per cent of people were found to consider the goal of owner-occupation desirable. Figures of tenure before the First World War are unreliable, but it is estimated that only 10 per cent of people owned their own homes (M. Swenarton and S. Taylor, *Economic History Review*, Vol 38, 1985, pp. 373–92). This would imply that 90 per cent rented from private landlords. Now only 8 per cent rent privately. We have the smallest private rented sector in the Western world.

Much of the rise in home ownership originated in nineteenth-century working-class traditions of self and mutual help. The old non-profit-making building clubs were formed by ordinary people to enable them to purchase their own houses, and they succeeded spectacularly, attracting very high levels of investment, and growing into the wealthy and diverse building societies and mortgage lenders of today, with their billions of pounds of assets. They financed the building boom of the 1930s which gave 1.8 million families the chance of buying new homes (most of which are still part of the housing stock), and the second, post-war boom brought in millions more. The British wanted to buy. Nobody was making them do it. They chose, freely, and continued to choose, to buy. No political party suggested that home ownership was evil or immoral. The rate of inflation in the massive price booms of 1971–3 and 1978–80 raised a few worried eyebrows, as well as making a lot of people richer, but it would be unfair to claim that more than a handful of the extremely committed on the left considered home ownership in itself a social or political crime. We do not often hear in this country the view that property is theft.

Similarly, all political parties from the end of the First World War onwards and for most of this century have accepted the need to provide public-sector housing for those who could not or did not wish to buy. As the private sector dwindled, so the public grew. It is true that the left tended to extol the virtues of council housing (fair rents, responsible and accountable landlords, collective spirit, neighbourliness, planned developments) more than the right, but nobody suggested that we could or should do without it.

Nor, in a sense, is it argued that we can do without it altogether now. (*Arguing*, with its suggestions of reasoned debate, would not be the word for the muddled process that has taken place.) But the climate has changed, and with the growth of privatisation attitudes towards public housing have changed profoundly. Home ownership is now being actively encouraged *at the expense not of the private but of the public sector.* Since the Right-to-Buy was announced in 1980, well over a million council houses have been sold at a discount: John Patten, then Housing Minister, announced the sale of the millionth in September 1986. Council houses had been sold to sitting tenants under previous governments (rising from an average of about 2000 a year in 1953, when a ban on sales was lifted, through the sixties, to 45,000 in 1972), but the figures of the last ten years are unprecedented. The majority of the tenants who bought are satisfied with their purchase of greater autonomy, greater privacy and an appreciating asset. Some, as we have seen, have come badly unstuck through unexpectedly high

interest rates, or unexpected illness or unemploy-
ment, but they are a small minority. These new
home owners, most of them recruited from the
more affluent council tenants, are patted on the
back and portrayed as resourceful, independent,
responsible. They have a stake in the country. They
cultivate their gardens. They care for their space.
They are good and active citizens. A moral approval
is extended to them as a class. Their tenant-
neighbours sometimes complain that their new
status makes them grow snobbish and stand-offish,
but it is probably only envy that speaks.

This is all very well, and one would not wish to
claim or even to imply by a turn of phrase that there
is anything wrong with home ownership, anything
unnatural or reactionary or antisocial. I myself
would go so far as to use a term that no sociologist
would risk, and say that the desire for a home of
one's own seems to me to be 'natural'. I have quite
a lot of home of my own and I am very attached to
all of it. I set an extremely high value on privacy
and the right to domestic eccentricity. I paid a lot
and worked hard for my property, it has appreciated,
it is mine, and I enjoy it. The act of possession and
its concomitant freedoms mean a lot to me, and I
do not know which of the satisfaction factors I have
mentioned I would rate highest if asked to fill in a
questionnaire (though I think I would place use
above capital). I feel sure my attitudes are not

unrepresentative. I have been a lodger in my time, I have been an insecure tenant, I have let my house, I have done a house-swap, I have had lodgers and the babies and boyfriends of lodgers living with me. And privacy is what I now want. I have become more territorial.

I used to be more critical of this need for privacy and private property, but I would now go along with the suspicion voiced to me by a justifiably houseproud neighbour at the beginning of the Thatcher era. As we chatted on his doorstep about graffiti, garbage, untended highrise council blocks, waste spaces and public ownership he, once a man of the left, voiced the opinion that 'What belongs to everybody belongs to nobody,' and to my surprise I found myself agreeing. He was, alas, right. Public squalor had set in with a vengeance in the black-bagged seventies, and the dream of public order and harmony and social fusion was perishing.

I was sad to see it go. Those who cannot remember that dream cannot imagine the sadness. We hoped society would move forward cheerfully into the future as an increasingly united and increasingly prosperous whole, not as a marching phalanx with devil-take-the-hindmost stragglers licking and mopping up the leftover trickle-down. We believed in levelling up. What went wrong? Did we get human nature wrong, or did we just get the sums wrong?

The architects of this failed Utopia are themselves saddened by what has happened. They have been turned from heroes into villains. Kenneth Campbell, Chief Housing Architect at the GLC from 1959–74, revisited the Le Corbusier-inspired estate at Roehampton, once a showpiece, and gazed at the communal neglect of the mid-eighties with depression, echoing my neighbour: 'Everybody's property is nobody's property.' He reminisced to Nicholas Shakespeare: 'We really thought that by putting families into this environment, they would change into ordinary middle-class families. The Scots, the French, the Americans all lived in highrises . . . The idea of having only four families to a floor was that they would be jolly good chums. They would talk to each other at the front door instead of at the garden fence. In fact, the only middle-class characteristic the tenants instantaneously acquired was non-neighbourliness' (Nicholas Shakespeare, *Londoners*, 1986). Alas for the buildings of Roehampton! They were celebrated as 'superb' by Nikolaus Pevsner (*The Englishness of English Art*, 1956), and serenaded as 'off-white Monet girls in an impressionist garden' by Reyner Banham (*A Personal View of Modern Architecture*, 1962). They are not as pure and innocent as once they were. The simple problem, as Nicholas Shakespeare puts it, is that nobody sweeps a common path.

Walking round many council estates in London one can see the truth of this dumped in every stairwell. The grimness and squalor of some of the London system-built highrise and deck-access estates are indescribable, though Salman Rushdie has a good try in a memorable passage on page 461 of *The Satanic Verses*, and J. G. Ballard in his roast-Alsatian science fiction nightmare *High Rise* gets the right flavour. Wander round for yourself and see. Nobody will eat you. These are your fellow citizens. Wander round the notorious Mozart near Paddington, or the Holly Street in Hackney, or the Aylesbury in south London, said to be the biggest estate in the world. Jagged broken windows stuffed with rags gape, yawning holes blackened by fire stare down angrily, and intersections on staircases are loaded with broken prams, dead beds, lumps of everlasting polystyrene, and old cookers. The lifts are adorned with everyday obscenities and insults, though one bears the arresting and remarkably literate exhortation, 'Suck your mother while she's having her period' – somebody there has learned the language and profited from it. Barricaded doors bear warnings about Fierce Guard Dogs. Spyholes peep suspiciously. Outside, refuse overflows from giant containers, and stray cats scavenge. In summer, it stinks. Atrocity stories about television sets hurled at visitors from eighteenth-floor balconies do not seem wholly implausible here.

I was taken round Broadwater Farm by a friend whose sister had lived there in its happier days, and indeed from the distance it still looms pleasantly, with some hints of architectural distinction. Somebody had worked hard at the drawing board. But from within, it is eerily lifeless by day, and one can see large public spaces one would not want to cross at night. I am told money has been spent on it since the tragic and brutal death of PC Blakelock in 1985. Walkways have been brightly painted and flowerbeds attempted. Kill a policeman and get your estate a facelift.

The notice in the window of the Hackney Housing Finance Centre tells its own story. 'For safety reasons we have to limit numbers in reception to 35 people. When we reach this figure we will close the doors and only reopen when it is safe to do so. Please wait/queue as hopefully this won't take long.' The Citizens' Advice Bureau across the road takes up the refrain: 'Due to severe shortages . . . we can only see the first 25 people at 10 am on Mondays and Thursdays.'

The gulf between owners and tenants is getting wider and wider. These estates are dumping grounds, where only those without choice end up – the poor, the unemployed, the single parents, the old, the black, the disadvantaged. These are the homes of the new underclass. The middle masses of the new property-owning democracy move on, leaving the rest behind. (Ralf Dahrendorf estimates the underclass at a conservative 5 per cent, a figure without electoral significance but with a fairly large capacity for human misery.) The growing divide and the new mystique reinforce the old coals-in-the-bath, live-like-pigs, them-and-us stereotypes of council tenants. These people are failures, they have lost out, or they wouldn't be living there, would they? The more you praise people for becoming home owners, the more you implicitly condemn those who are not.

Up north, in Sheffield, life is not quite so unequal or so grim. The most visible and ill-famed highrise blocks (the architecture of which, despite all, I along with Reyner Banham have admired) are currently being converted into accommodation for the World Student Games of 1991, and then some will be rebuilt as lowrise traditional pitched-roof housing. It is a partnership scheme, and not all the units built will belong to the council. Local authorities now have severe restrictions placed upon their ability to finance conversions or new building. (They are obliged to sell to tenants, cannot spend the income on more houses, have a statutory obligation to house the homeless, and are forbidden to borrow to build. The logic, I repeat, seems odd.) There are some attractively designed new-build partnership schemes in the pipeline, part council rental, part housing association rental or shared-ownership, part for sale into the private sector. On a sunny day in May, a stroll through the estates at Manor Park or Wincobank or Parsons Cross or Mosborough is pleasant. The views from the low-rise new homes at Skye Edge or the highrise old homes at Norfolk Park are glorious.

But why is it that the little local shops, even on the most pleasant estates, are so mean and shabby? Some are empty, many are boarded up. Why cannot local shopkeepers make a better living? Why the barricades, the locks, the grids, the cardboard?

By daytime, nobody looks violent. People stop to chat and gossip. 'How are you, love? Nice to see you, duck. Can I help you, love? Who are you looking for? Why don't you try the back stairs?' I paused to admire a particularly beautiful garden, overflowing with clematis and roses and aubrietia. I summoned up courage to tap nervously on the door. 'I just wanted to say how much I liked your garden,' I said to the elderly woman in her kitchen, embarrassed to intrude on her private space. 'Oh, thank you,' she said. 'There's many that say so. He had a letter, from someone saying how much she'd enjoyed it . . . Of course, he has more time for the garden now. Yes, we bought the house. A couple of years ago, we bought the house. But the council let him do what he liked with the garden, even before that. There was a time when they wouldn't, you know. When you had to have it all the same. But now, they let you do it your own way.'

The house next door was empty, being redecorated. I peered through its windows. When I returned to the street, a woman waiting at the bus stop who had been watching my adventures said eagerly, 'Are you going to take it?' I said it was very nice, and offered her a lift home. In the car, she encouraged me. 'Go on, go to the council and put your name down. It's a lovely house. If you get it, come and have a cup of coffee with me. My son lives round the corner there. Come in and have a coffee now, why don't you? I must have just missed that bus, thanks for the lift, I'd been waiting a while. Do go and put your name down, love.'

An innocent tenant, she. Those on the waiting list for renting on the desirable estates can wait for ten years, for fifteen years, forever. Alan Wigfield, Chair of Housing in Sheffield, remembers the good old days when you could go down to queue at the housing office in the morning and be given a key for a flat on the desirable Gleadless Estate four hours later. No longer.

Government cuts, restrictions on spending, and Right-to-Buy have affected the whole country. According to a recent report in the *Guardian*, no new council homes were built in 1989 in Nottingham, Liverpool, Bradford, Plymouth, Portsmouth and Southampton, and in several London boroughs. In my own borough of Camden, which receives an influx of homeless from three mainline stations and has over 1500 official homeless households on its books, only thirty-one new units were built in 1989/90 and none are planned for 1991. The cost of renting in the private sector in Camden is astronomical. The cost of land in Camden is astronomical. The Bed and Breakfast places bulge, and so do the council hostels. The number of the homeless, increases. So where are people to live? Where are they to go, those who cannot exercise the Right-to-Buy or even the right to rent?

They can always sleep on the streets, of course. The dossers and vagrants of Camden are on the move, according to the *Hampstead and Highgate Express* (18 May 1990), making their way north from King's Cross and the Euston Road to 'the leafy heights' of Hampstead and Highgate. London's cardboard city, familiar to hurrying intruders on their way to the National Theatre or the Festival Hall or Waterloo Station, has many little suburbs now. Visitors from countries where they do things differently are amazed to stumble across them. Walking along The Strand at 10.45 one night in May, I notice that almost every shop entrance has its occupant, some silver-haired and already bedded down for the night, some young and chatting. 'You know, you can get nicked for begging,' says one young man, seriously, to another. I give a pound to

23

a couple of boys squatting between Kentucky Fried Chicken and your friendly mortgage lender, Abbey National plc. We'll spend it on food, they politely and perhaps truthfully promise. One of the official private-sector gentlemen I interviewed in the course of my research described his reaction to this new street phenomenon. Coming out of a black-tie dinner for the Building Societies Association or some such important body at the Savoy, he'd seen them there, in their little campsites. And he'd thought they were having quite a good time. Quite a lot of fun. He spoke almost with envy. His remarks were rather sad, on more levels than one.

The young Samuel Johnson and the penniless poet Savage sometimes walked the streets all night, arm-in-arm, when they hadn't the money even for a doss house. It sounds romantic now. Johnson survived, but Savage died in a debtors' prison. Johnson, a man of the greatest kindness, did not forget.

An old-style tramp called round at my door last winter. I was just in the process of recording a radio interview with a Swedish journalist about the state of Britain. The tramp – one of those ageless Irish gentlemen somewhere between thirty and seventy – wanted to sweep up the leaves from my front garden. The Swedish interviewer gave him a pound. I gave him a pound. He went off and swept up the leaves. Then he rang the bell and asked if I had a sleeping bag to spare. He was sleeping in the hospital car park and it was getting nippy. I went off to look, failed to find a bag, and gave him a blanket. The Swedish interviewer meanwhile had donated another coin. Five minutes later, he rang again. His boots were muddy. Could I give him some water? They were good boots, he didn't want to ruin them. I went off and found a knife, a brush and a bucket, and we did our best with the heavy London clay. He thanked us, and off he went into the night. The Swedish interviewer got a good interview. Did such things happen often, she wanted to know? No, I said, truthfully. Not often. Occasionally. And in Sweden? Oh, never. Never.

I had a good bit of journalistic luck myself on my visit to St Mungo's, the charity that raises funds for and provides direct-access hostels for the homeless. As I was working out how on earth to cross the impossible stretch of motorway near Paddington that calls itself the Harrow Road, I saw a dead man on the pavement. I didn't realise he was dead, I thought he was just sitting there in a slumped heap, but then an ambulance came up and put him on a stretcher and covered his face with a sort of tea towel. They wouldn't have done that if he hadn't been dead, would they? I wanted to stare, but I was too polite. I'll never make an investigative journalist.

So, there are the anecdotes. You say you want statistics. In this area, they are hard to collect, but

Mick Carroll of St Mungo's estimates that about 10,000 sleep rough in London every night.

And how do the homeless link up with the home owners and their mortgages? Are the new home owners responsible for their plight? Surely not, you will say.

No, it is the government which is responsible. The government has turned home ownership into a mystique, and has failed to provide for those who cannot or will not subscribe to it. The government, which says it believes in choice, has diminished choice. Over the past ten years, tenants and would-be tenants have seen their options dwindle and become more unacceptable as a result of *deliberate government policy*. The homeless on the streets are merely the visible reminders of the hundreds of thousands on waiting lists up and down the country.

What does the government think will be the end result of this determined favouring of owners over tenants? Why is it preventing local authorities from maintaining, let alone from increasing, its housing stock? Is it a *political plot*? Is it a conspiracy to make everyone vote Tory forever in order to defend their stake in the country? (We all suspect, and research has tended to confirm, that home owners are more likely to vote Tory than tenants or disenfranchised tramps.) Did Nicholas Ridley mean it when he hinted that he would like to see the public sector dwindle to nothing? Does Junior Housing Minister

Christopher Chope really think that the twin problems of crippling mortgage repayments for home owners and nowhere to live for tenants can be significantly ameliorated by the former taking in the latter as 'informal lodgers', living 'as members of the household'? Into those first-time buy, £60,000 studio flats?) (*World at One*, BBC4, 24 April 1990.)

Let us look, for a moment, at the private landlord. As we have seen, private tenancies in this country have shrunk over the last few decades to a tiny percentage. This has happened through a series of regulations brought in by different governments. Like estate agents, private landlords usually get a bad press – they are extortionate, uncaring, unresponsive, absentee, and if they want to get rid of you, they harass you. (It is well to remember, though, that Shirley Green, biographer of Peter Rachman, the slum landlord of the sixties who gave his name to Rachmanism, found that many Notting Hill blacks spoke up for the folk monster – at least he let rooms to them, even if he screwed them. No one else would. West Indian social worker: 'Don't expect me to run the man down . . . To the West Indian he was a saviour and a lot of people still have a lot of respect for him.' *Rachman*, 1979.)

This government has tried to revive the private sector by such schemes as the Business Expansion Scheme (described by those hostile to it as 'a tax-break for property speculators'), but has not yet achieved much widespread success. Anyway, the BES tends to cater for the upper end of the rental market, as the Tory-led London Boroughs Association, while welcoming the initiative, conceded (*Giving Hope to London's Homeless – The Way Forward*, May 1989). Even at the upper end, landlords find it hard to make a profit. And it is unlikely that the private sector will ever again help to provide low-cost housing. Rich and professional people, apart from a migrant minority like diplomats, film stars and academics, don't want to rent, and why should anyone, even with an incentive, go in for renting to the poor who subsist on government-fixed Housing Benefit? There is no profit to be squeezed out of Housing Benefit.

Being a landlord is a mug's game. Why should businessmen or financiers be philanthropists? Why should anyone go in for such a thankless task as letting to low-income families, or, God forbid, the unemployed? There is simply no money in it. I am not being ironic. I really cannot see why anyone should expect private individuals or companies to take on the responsibilities of managing rented property for less of a return on their money than they can get in other easier, more conventional ways. Property is a headache. Keeping one's own roof intact is bad enough. Tenants are a headache. They are litigious, unpredictable, they keep illicit pets and cut cat-doors in your woodwork, they will not leave when you want, they prevent you from selling your property when the market is right, and sometimes they will not pay up.

You have to be crazy to be a small-scale private landlord. I know of one who hasn't collected the rent on a block in south London for years because he just can't be bothered. The house next door to me used to belong to an elderly would-be novelist who let bedsits to students and nurses: he harassed them with unwanted attentions and me with unwanted manuscripts, and his idea of keeping down the weeds in the garden was to cover it with old carpets. He spent a lot of time trying to fix things on the cheap, but nothing ever quite worked. I know a philanthropic chap in north London who owns a huge empire of highly desirable properties, lets at reasonable rents and will always turn up with an efficient screwdriver when needed. When two or three of Mr G's tenants are gathered together, they spend all their time discussing why he is so crazy and so unbusinesslike and which of them should write his memoirs. He could sell up for millions. Does he *like* wandering around with a screwdriver? Perhaps he is a saint. But you can't count on there being any more saints where he came from.

No, the age of the private landlord, with the odd eccentric exception, is over. As Peter Saunders writes, 'Given the long-standing hostility of governments, it is now extremely doubtful whether individuals can ever again be induced to invest in rental housing' (*A Nation of Home Owners*, 1990, p.23). And profit-seeking institutions cannot be tempted back either. So where does that leave the would-be tenant? By and large, back in the diminishing public sector, now up for sale.

There are, of course, the housing associations, and partnership schemes, and shared-ownership schemes, which seem to offer some way out of the impasse. They have come into their own in the past decade. They are smiled upon by government and supported by grants and expertise through the Housing Corporation. They aim to offer low-cost housing for a range of clients – for the elderly, for first-time shared-ownership buyers, for young singles and young families. There has been a wide range of initiatives, ranging from the Paddington Churches Housing Association, founded twenty-five years ago, which has managed thousands of lets from otherwise reluctant private landlords to homeless families, to Woolwich Homes Limited, an offshoot of the Woolwich Building Society established in 1983 'to provide good-quality, well-designed, affordable housing', particularly for first-time buyers and the elderly. A recent new-build Woolwich development at Sidcup (opened June 1990) will provide fifty homes, some for sale, some for rent, and some for sale with shared equity

– the Woolwich has taken a lead in devising imaginative new 'mechanisms' for working with local authorities and housing associations, and claims 'our business is housing, not just owner-occupation' (Trevor Baker, Managing Director, Woolwich Homes).

The long-established Notting Hill Housing Trust has gone in both for renovation and new build, for small schemes and large. It has rescued some areas of dramatic and colourful urban blight and turned them into little enclaves of brightly-painted, light-reflecting, cunningly contrived domestic delight. The area known as 'Frestonia', which delcared UDI when it was squatted by the Bramley Housing Co-op, has been transformed, with consultation, into eighty-six new rented homes and thirty homes for the elderly. The Norland Road Scheme, funded by the Housing Corporation, is just yards from the Shepherds Bush motorway and it is so unexpectedly handsome that it takes the breath away.

There are housing association enterprises all over the country, not all of them urban. I'd hardly noticed them before, but now I see them everywhere. In a deep lost valley in Somerset, three lambs bleat insistently through a fence at Tarr Water Cottages, built by the Knightstone Housing Association and opened, as a plaque announces, in July 1988. On 6 June 1990 I attended a turf-cutting ceremony in

31

Porlock for a project to build twenty-seven homes for local people, to rent and to buy: the project is a shared enterprise between West Somerset Rural Housing Association and English Villages Housing Association.

There are, of course, much larger projects in urban areas. The attractively landscaped and sited Flower Estate in Wincobank, Sheffield, is also a new-build mixed development, the result of a partnership between the Council and the United Kingdom Housing Trust which hopes to provide 2000 new homes in the area. (Of course 'attractive' is a comparative term: when I mentioned that I'd liked the look of the development to a Rotherham estate agent, he was somewhat dismissive. What, with the M1 in hearing and an industrial, not a rural, view?)

So, are housing trusts the government's answer to its own problem? Not quite, it seems. They are simply not wealthy enough to cope with the shortfall. In the whole of rural Cornwall, in a year, twenty new homes were built. And that, said the National Agricultural Centre Rural Trust, was a good year. Next year won't be so good. The Housing Corporation has run out of money. Some of the earlier council-trust deals have now been made illegal: the Flower Estate got through on a late-night emergency council meeting just before the law changed, and it is widely believed that government opposition to this kind of deal springs from ingrained ideological distrust of local authorities. The government remains committed to its 'overriding principle that everything should be for sale'. What this means is that however hard wicked local authorities and saintly housing associations work to get together and to provide new rented accommodation, they have been in most circumstances obliged to sell on. Housing associations have lobbied hard to protect their properties, and have been in some measure successful – over the tea and cream cakes at Porlock it was stressed that 'legal controls' would ensure the buildings remained available at a subsidised price to local people even when they changed hands. But many associations have been and still are building, in effect, for the private sector. Their subsidies are being sold on. In some villages, the only land likely to be available for building for a hundred years has been allocated to housing trusts, then sold on into the private sector.

Does this matter, so long as somebody is living in the new houses? Could we not conclude that, as most people want to own anyway, it would be a Good Thing if all housing ended up in the private sector? This is perhaps what the government would like. Sometimes it seems to think that home ownership is innately so desirable that nobody should want to rent. And those who insist, for reasons of poverty or stubbornness or the right to choose, on remaining tenants, should opt to be the tenants of private landlords. (Many now have that option extended, through the Tenants' Choice scheme, which has certainly had the useful effect of making some of the less competent local authorities brush up their estates.)

I would like to argue that there is a lasting need for reasonable rented accommodation under responsible management, be it by local authority or housing trust. Most experts agree that a 70 per cent level of home ownership is about saturation point for the nation, and of the remaining 30 per cent of the equation, many, particularly the young and the elderly, would, given an attractive range of possibilities, *prefer* to rent. At the moment their needs are being brutally ignored.

It is reasonable to assume that at least some young people are driven into premature purchases by lack of rented choice. Young people are generally less territorial than the middle-aged. They do not want to tie themselves down to a job or a neighbourhood for life, nor is it wholly good for the nation if they do. Mobility is good for the economy, as Norman Tebbit told us. It is often argued that one of the problems with local-authority housing is that it creates immobility, and this is true, but so, of course, does ownership.

Young people expect to leave the parental home

and set up on their own at an increasingly early age, for various reasons, and whatever they are told about the virtues of family life this trend is unlikely to change. (Except, perhaps, in one statistically insignificant but sociologically interesting pocket, in which permissive middle-class parents find twenty-plus-year-olds hanging on longer and longer in the comforts of a free and tolerant home. Such parents, as Jill Tweedie recently reported, may well find themselves yelling at their over-affectionate offspring, 'What's wrong with a card-board box?')

Many of these young people would like to rent. Many do. They like sharing, and are good at creating informal co-operative arrangements. Young couples with children begin to feel a need for more security and privacy – though here I go along with the femin-ist, anti-home-base argument that many young mothers often get more privacy than they want – but many do not want to settle down before they have to. The home-ownership mystique and its effect on both house prices and rent levels is threatening the natural experimentalism of the young. We are be-coming a nation of young fogeys. That may be good for the Tory vote, but is it really good for us?

I well remember moving into this house on my first mortgage more than twenty years ago. I sat down on the green wall-to-wall second-hand carpet (very Cyril Lord, murmured a sardonic bachelor friend): I sat amidst the packing cases and wept. I was afraid – afraid of my mortgage payments, afraid of my rates, afraid of the gamble I'd taken on my freelance income, afraid that I was about to turn into a dull bourgeoise worrier mortgaged to Grub Street. No more sitting on the pavement in The Strand, no more wandering hand-in-hand for me. Well, I paid off the mortgage (laughably low by modern standards), but who knows, maybe I did turn into somebody else in the process? Buying a house isn't like buying a saucepan or three-piece suite. It changes you.

Is it not possible that all this putting of money in bricks and mortar locks up not only our financial futures but our imaginations? Are there not other, more exciting, more socially constructive, more forward-looking, more entertaining ways of investing one's money and creating one's future? Houses may be safe, but they are very inert. At my age, so am I, but it wasn't always so. We are an ageing nation. We are frightened of risk. Houses are safe, let us stick with them. It is argued that we now expect to make more money (whatever that phrase means) from our home ownership than from our working lives. Our life chances are improved more by buying our homes than by our life's work. (And diminished more by not owning than by not working.) Am I alone in finding the implications of this alarming?

(If we take another look at Matthew 25 and the parable of the talents, most frequently invoked by the left, we may well come up with a different and slightly confusing interpretation: the one-talent man who buries his money in the ground could perhaps be likened to the home owner who feels that owning is safer than doing, and who will take no risks with his capital. His house happens to appreciate, but only because of the otherwise de-plored rate of inflation. His savings are safe in the building society, where they fuel inflation, rather than build new homes. The parable is deeply am-biguous.)

So, there are the problems. Too many homeless, not enough rented accommodation, a growing financial and social gap between owners and ren-ters, and a possible threat through the temptation of inertia to the whole future of British investment. Now we come to the answers. This is always the tricky bit.

On the investment/inertia front, David Blunkett argues that a Labour government could through tax incentives encourage social investment in local industry. Instead of tamely putting one's money in a building society, one could invest it in an Industrial Society, which would provide not only a return on capital but also a stimulus to the local economy. He has talked to German bankers about the way such schemes operate in Germany, and believes there are opportunities here, if only we were not so committed to short-term gain rather than long-term growth. And the building societies themselves could be encouraged in their more imaginative long-term projects.

There have been some interesting proposals for bettering the lot of tenants. Brian Walden, recognising the growing gulf between owner and non-owner, disarmingly suggested that council tenants who cannot buy should be given their homes (*Sunday Times*, 29 May 1988). I applaud the generous spirit of this, though I cannot feel it would go down well with the mortgaged neighbours. More practical, perhaps, are various schemes for converting rent into mortgage payments. And it is good to note that the somewhat anarchical spirit of self-building is still very much alive. But however high the rate of home ownership rises, everyone I met who works in the field believes there will still be a perfectly proper need for reasonable rented accommodation, and for socially responsible management. Only the government appears to deny this.

Estates do not manage themselves, just as public roads do not sweep or police themselves. We should recognise, and respect, the work of management, just as we respect (well, used to respect) doctors, teachers and policemen, and other professionals and public servants. Some local authorities have been good landlords, some have been bad, just as some private landlords have been good, some bad. At the moment all of them feel insulted, threatened and demoralised. All of them feel as though they have been kicked in the teeth. It is time to recognise that the profit motive and the free market will never house those on Housing Benefit. We need to restore the confidence and self-respect both of tenants and landlords. The vulgar and childish abuse which the present government pours upon local authorities must come to an end. It is painful and embarrassing to witness. The financial restrictions which prevent local authorities from housing their tenants properly must be reviewed. People are suffering because of a misplaced ideological commitment to the free market. In housing, the free market will not work. Tenants are not criminals. They too have rights.

And let us lessen their present handicap by abolishing MITR, or by phasing it out as painlessly as possible. Everybody but Mrs Thatcher agrees that it is a nonsense, although some of them dare not say so. Indeed, the whole housing subsidy system is, in Peter Saunders' words, 'confused, expensive, contradictory and biased' (*A Nation of Home Owners*). At present, as we have seen, it is grossly biased towards the owner, and removal of MITR would go some way to redressing the balance. It would also check inflation of house prices, as Nigel Lawson's decision in August 1988 showed, and would thus help young first-time buyers, who have perhaps suffered most from the present system. The Labour Party has committed itself to retaining relief but will restrict it to the standard rate and withdraw extra relief for those on higher rates of tax. This is a step in the right direction, but it doesn't go far enough.

Nobody is going to do anything much about anything on the housing front before the next election – a few hostel beds here and there, in empty hospitals and church halls, perhaps, to clean up the streets for the tourists, but nothing substantial. Now is the time to start thinking ahead about how to sort out the whole subsidy muddle. One interesting proposal, for a unitary needs-related housing allowance, was put forward in the 1985 Inquiry Into British Housing, chaired by the Duke of Edinburgh. It would have been, in housing jargon, 'tenure-neutral' – in other words it would have favoured neither tenant nor owner. It would have been targeted wholly at need. It was greeted with respect, and then forgotten. It was a long-term plan, and nobody is interested in the long term. Nobody dares offend the electorate of the property-owning democracy. We play it safe.

Surely now is the time to decide what sort of housing balance we need and want for the future. I have argued that we need and want a rented sector, and that some of that will remain in the public sector. But whether it is public, private or partnership, now is the time to recognise with generosity of spirit and finance the continuing need for low-cost social housing and high-quality, well-paid managers.

And now is the time to ask ourselves seriously whether we want to encourage or discourage the inflation of property prices. I cannot believe that the inflation spiral is healty, either psychologically or financially, yet every day I seem to hear some pundit telling us that a rise in house prices will be good news. I even heard someone say it would be good news for first-time buyers. That is rubbish. He didn't mean 'first-time buyers', he meant 'first-time boughters'. Many first-time buyers will never get a look-in, if the rest of us have our way. Kick the ladder away behind you, and grow fat. Can we seriously want a future of cheaper mortgages and dearer houses?

Is there something in our society that really *wants* to gloat over its appreciating bricks and mortar while others sleep on the street? Of course not, you indignantly reply. The homeless, you will tell me, are an over-publicised, over-glamorised, statistically insignificant group, most of whom get exactly what they are asking for. They are merely 'symbolic'.

I agree. It is what they symbolise that we should address: the unseen, the unvisited, the unrepresented, ill housed in bed-and-breakfasts, in rotten rented accommodation, on council waiting lists. Are they also getting what they are asking for, do you think? Are they getting what they deserve? Do you really think they are all victims of wicked local authorities? Are they not rather the victims of our subsidised greed?

About the Author

MARGARET DRABBLE is a well-known novel-
ist and critic, and the editor of *The Oxford Companion
to English Literature*. Her novels include *The
Millstone*, *The Middle Ground*, *The Radiant Way* and
A Natural Curiosity

CHATTO

Counter*Blasts*

Also available in bookshops now:-

Forthcoming CounterBlasts (and Specials) will include Shirley Hazzard on Waldheim and the United Nations, and Brenda Maddox on the Pope and birth control.

If you want to join in the debate, and if you want to know more about **Counter*Blasts*,** the writers and the issues, then write to:

Random Century Group, Freepost 5066, Dept MH, London SW1V 2YY